Empowerment And Encouragement for Living in a Fallen World

Donna Louis

Dedications

To God, my heavenly father, who continues to lead and guide my steps. Thank you for pouring into me and keeping the anointing on me 24/7 365.

To my tremendous husband of forty years, Patrick. You have stuck with me through thick and thin and the highs and lows of my career always encouraging me when I wanted to give up and give in. I love you.

ISBN: 979-8-9855174-3-9

Contents

Introduction   VII

1. Serving   1

2. Humility   3

3. Forgiveness   7

4. Patience   11

5. Gratitude   15

6. Peace   19

7. Love   25

8. Empowerment Quotes   39

About the Author   41

Acknowledgements   45

Other Books By Donna Louis   47

Introduction

"Mayday, Mayday, Mayday" we are going down! This is what pilots say when they are in a distress situation with their plane. The entire world is in a distress situation now more than ever.

There are wars, political unrest, inflation, racism, climate change, murders, and a host of other evils taking place. This is not the way God intended his world to be when he created it. Things were so simple back in the Garden of Eden until temptation and sin came to life.

Why is all of this happening? It's very simple we are living in a fallen world. God created all his people to love one another as he loves us and to live in peace. He gave us dominion over everything and instead of caring for it, we are destroying everything!

Instead of being humble, we are so prideful. Instead of loving each other, we are spewing hatred every chance we get. God said he is a jealous God, and we are to have no other gods before him. Well, the idolatry list is endless of all the things we place a higher priority on instead of God. Money. sex sins, a big house, luxury car, fashionable clothes, a big enough budget for luxury travel, an attractive spouse, lots of children (some of you don't even know how you are going to care for them) you just know you want them so when you get old, they can care for you. Sounds a little selfish. What about their futures and what they want to do? Some of you are looking to have your own starting five, like in the NBA.

Then there are the more elaborate material desires, like owning a yacht. Not saying that this is something you shouldn't dream about, but have you thought about the cost? The fuel it will take to run it, the maintenance and upkeep charge, what is the docking fee to keep it in the marina and, depending on the size of it, the salary for the crew to take you back and forth?

These are nice things, but if you place them above God, you are living life upside down. I enlightened you in one of my previous books, "Book of Proverbs–Proverbs for the Modern Day," that this warped thinking is not good for you. The bottom line is when you go, these things are not going with you, especially money. I don't care what arrangements you make with the funeral director; it is not going to work out in your favor. And you are totally not getting anything to go with you if you are cremated!

When Jesus was here on earth, he gave us some tremendous examples of how we should live, and it hasn't changed just because it's the 21st century!

The Lord has given me seven examples of biblical characters from the Bible that followed his example, and we all should do the same. So, buckle your seatbelt and let's get started.

Chapter 1
Serving

Mary–The Listener

When Jesus was here on earth, he was an excellent listener. Jesus' listening skills were characterized by empathy, attentiveness, and curiosity. Jesus was very interested in people's lives, interests, and needs. When Jesus was around his disciples especially, he listened to their doubts, fears, and questions, and provided them with guidance and clarity of mind.

Mary, the sister of Lazarus, followed Jesus' example. In Luke Chapter 10:38-42 when Jesus was visiting Mary and her sister Martha, who was Lazarus's sisters, Martha was busy serving all the people who were there and became very upset with Mary because she wasn't helping her. Martha was doing what was proper custom and manners by attending to her guests. Martha approached Jesus with her plight and was surprised that Jesus told her that what Mary was doing by sitting at his feet and listening was more important that Martha serving her guests.

Luke 10:38-42

King James Version

Now it came to pass, as they went, that he entered a certain village, and a certain woman named Martha received him into her house.

And she had a sister called Mary, which also sat at Jesus' feet, and heard his word.

But Martha was cumbered about much serving, and came to him, and said, Lord, dost thou not care that my sister hath left me to serve alone? Bid her therefore that she help me.

And Jesus answered and said unto her, Martha, Martha, thou art careful and troubled about many things:

But one thing is needful: and Mary hath chosen that good part, which shall not be taken away from her.

Basically, what Jesus was telling Martha is that it was more important to listen to him than to her serving her guests. (For those of you that watch WWE Wrestling, I will put this in terms you can understand clearly. When Jesus was saying listen to me is the same as when Roman Reigns says to the crowd "Acknowledge Me."

However, let me give you the clearest example: you are to listen twice as much as you speak or do. That is why God gave us all two ears and one mouth. Martha was quick to say to Jesus, speak to Mary, and get her to help me. Her talking fell on deaf ears. "When there are many words, sin is unavoidable, but the one who controls his lips is prudent."–Proverbs 10:19 CSB

If we are to duplicate Jesus, we need to be good listeners. John Maxwell, the greatest leadership teacher with his books, says, "There is no quicker way to earn respect as a leader than being slow to speak. It is called listening, and it plays a big role in what I call "The Law of Connection." How will you know what is important to people unless you ask and listen to the answers? If you prove to be a leader who solicits feedback and pays attention to what's being said, then you will earn your connection and your followers will respect the guidance you give."

Duplicate Jesus be a listener.

Chapter 2
Humility

Moses–The Obedient One

Humility definition KJV Bible dictionary - In ethics, freedom from pride and arrogance, humbleness of mind a modest estimate of one's own worth. In theology, humility consists in a lowliness of mind, a deep sense of one's own unworthiness in the sight of God, self-abasement, penitence for sin, and submission to the divine will. Before honor is humility.

Humility is not attractive. Humility is hard.

When we think about humility, we see images surface about allowing other people to walk all over us. We have difficulty accepting praise. We also suffer with negative thinking that we must reject wealth, affirmation, even love. We access in our minds that humble people don't require those things. Then we think, who would want to be humble if it means living a life of despair and desolation?

We let negativity run rampart and allow stinking thinking to take over. Our minds say that wealth prevents people from getting to heaven. We think that those who want to follow Jesus have to let everything go. We believe we can only be successful in the world or humble and destitute. We believe that being humble means that allowing your desires, hopes, dreams, and plans to wither away and die and allowing God to do whatever he wants to do with you will only keep you in survival mode or even lower. This is dangerous thinking because the bible clearly states, "The thief cometh not, but for to steal, and to kill, and to destroy: I am come that they might have life, and that they might have it more abundantly."–John 10:10. – KJV.

From time to time, we all look at ourselves in the mirror and see only flaws and disgracefulness. please keep in mind those negative thoughts come from Satan himself because the Bible says, "For we are God's masterpiece. He has created us anew in Christ Jesus, so we can do the good things he planned for us long ago."–Ephesians 2:10. – NLT.

"Humility is not thinking less of yourself but thinking of yourself less."–G. K. Chesterton.

When we reject humility, we embrace pride. then, at that point, we believe we are the masters of our own destiny. When we reject and ignore humility, then we are imprisoning ourselves. Pride leads to a host of other sins that ultimately bring out our selfishness and then the danger begins because then we believe we can treat people as puppets and use them to our advantage. We also puff up our chests and say that our gifts, talents, successes, and accomplishments are due to ourselves. The bible clearly states, "Yes, I am the vine; you are the branches. Those who remain in me, and I in them, will produce much fruit. For apart from me, you can do nothing."–John 15:5. – NIV.

"Humility is nothing but truth, and pride is nothing but lying."–St. Vincent De Paul.

God created us in his own image, but we are not our own saviors and with that in mind, we cannot escape death. Even Jesus could not escape it.

If we desire to live successful lives and have that transmit into every area of our lives (career, marriage, friendships) we must recognize that it all starts with an intimate relationship with God and that humility is the major factor. God created us, not us thinking that we created him. We were all given our own set of fingerprints and with that; we are authentic and being authentically humble doesn't mean that success is evil.

In our journey of life with Jesus, humility is essential. Humility sets us in a right relationship with God. Once we discipline ourselves to humility, it actually produces confidence and raises our self-esteem.

Having desires in life is not evil. It is when our desires become distorted that we cause ourselves much hardship and pull away from humility and God. Let's use the example of wanting to be loved. All of us want to be loved, but when we will do anything to make it happen, then the good desire works against us.

If we desire to have humility, we will need to redefine what that means. We need to look closely at some aspects of Jesus that may be new to us. We have to pinpoint the areas we struggle in, as well as the areas where we can grow. If you are willing and open to gaining humility, please recognize that this is a journey and don't expect perfection soon! On this journey, you will peel back layers of pride and aspiring to replace them with a humble spirit. God is doing a great work in all of us and gaining humility is just allowing that great work to take place.

Humility is key to obedience in God's mind, and Moses was the epitome of that. Moses obeyed God's commands and was so concerned that he could not be all God wanted him to be and execute the call on his life that he boldly told God, "But Moses said to the Lord, "My Lord, I've never been able to speak well, not yesterday, not the day before, and certainly not now since you've been talking to your servant. I have a slow mouth and a thick tongue." Exodus 4:9-11 CEB. Then the anger of the Lord burned against Moses, and He said, "Is there not your brother Aaron the Levite? I know that he speaks fluently. And behold, he is coming out to meet you; when he sees you, he will be overjoyed. So, you are to speak to him and put the words in his mouth; and I Myself will be with your mouth and his mouth, and I will instruct you in what you are to do. He shall speak for you to the people; and he will be as a mouth for you, and you will be as God to him. "–Exodus 4:14-16 NASB

Moses obeyed the call on his life and God was with him and did miraculous feats with Moses and he could lead the children of Israel out of bondage in Egypt from Pharoah.

Because of Moses' humble ways, the Bible says, "And there arose not a prophet since in Israel like unto Moses, whom the Lord knew face to face." - Deuteronomy 34:10

Having an intimate relationship with God and being a humble person will abundantly bless your life.

Chapter 3
Forgiveness

Jospeh–The Dreamer

"Imagination is everything. It is the preview of life's coming attractions."–Albert Einstein.

How many of you have dreams and have allowed them to die? It's never too late to chase your dreams. Some say that the richest place in the world is the cemetery. Why? Because of all the dreams, gifts, and talents that God placed in people, they allowed to go dormant and never let them blossom. Why? Dream stealers (people who were envious and told them they could never do it and they listened), fear, age, and a host of other negative thoughts. There are countless people who achieved their dreams late in life. The key is to believe and never give up, no matter what adversity comes your way. If Jesus had to deal with adversity and challenges when he was here on earth, what makes us exempt?

Bertha Wood was 90 years old when she started writing her first and only book (Fresh air and fun: the story of a Blackpool Holiday Camp) and it was published when she was 100 before she died at 101.

Harland Sanders was 65 before he had success with his first Kentucky Fried Chicken restaurant. https://www.inc.com/bill-murphy-jr/14-inspiring-people -who-found-crazy-success-later-in-life.html

Duncan Hines, at 73, licensed the right to use his name to the company that developed Duncan Hines Cake Mixes. https://www.inc.com/bill-murphy-jr/1 4-inspiring-people-who-found-crazy-success-later-in-life.html

Samuel Jackson, the actor, did not have success until he was 46 when he played in the movie Pulp Fiction along with John Travolta. https://www.inc.com/bill -murphy-jr/14-inspiring-people-who-found-crazy-success-later-in-life.html

All the above listed people encountered a lot of challenges, trials, & struggles before their dreams came to light, but they persevered and trusted God that he would make their dreams a reality.

This is what Joseph did as well. God gave him the dream that he would be a powerful leader, and his family would bow down to him, but it took an excruciating 13 years before that happened.

Joseph's brothers were very jealous of him when he told them his dream that they would bow down to him. He was the youngest of all the brothers, and his father loved him the most. Joseph's father Jacob sent him to go check on his brothers and when they saw Joseph coming, they threw him down into a ditch and planned to tell their father a wild animal killed him. However, when a caravan of Midianites came through town, the brothers pulled him out of the ditch and sold him into slavery.

Joseph found himself in a foreign country where he didn't speak the language. He was taken to Egypt and became a steward of a man named Potiphar, one of Pharoah's officials. Now Potiphar's wife had an eye for Joseph, and she tried to seduce him, and he ran from her. She complained to her husband and Jospeh was put in jail.

While in jail, he interpreted a couple of dreams for two people and when they were released, one promised him to speak to Pharoah about him but he never did and so he remained in prison.

One night Pharoah had a puzzling dream where he could not sleep, and he called for people to interpret the dream but none of them could. Finally, the person who was released from jail quite a while back remembered Joseph and spoke to Pharoah about him. The Pharoah called for Joseph; he interpreted the dream and Pharoah promoted him and made his second in command in Egypt under him.

Joseph oversaw all the food in the land because there was going to be seven years of plenty and seven years of famine. This was the interpretation of the dream.

The famine stretched all over the land, and Jacob and his sons had no food. Jacob advised his sons to go to Egypt and buy food. When they went, Jospeh recognized them, but they did not know this was the brother they sold.

After a few encounters Joseph revealed himself to his brothers who were frightened and scared that he would do harm to them, but Joseph told them, "As for you, you meant evil against me, but God meant it for good, to bring it about that many people should be kept alive, as they are this day."–Genesis 50:20. – AMP. Joseph had the brothers go back home and bring all their family members and his father Jacob and provided land and houses for all of them.

What a powerful story of forgiveness. I'm sure there are a lot of us that would have handled this differently and made our family members pay for their evil deeds. The Bible says, "if possible, as far as it depends on you, live at peace with everyone. Beloved, never avenge yourselves, but leave the way open for God's wrath (and His judicial righteousness]; for it is written [in Scripture], "Vengeance is Mine, I will repay," says the Lord. But if your enemy is hungry, feed him; if he is thirsty, give him a drink; for by doing this you will heap burning coals on his head."–Romans 12:18-20. - AMPC

One of the most repeated sermons in churches today is to have forgiveness. Is it easy? Definitely not. People decided whether to forgive people according to the severity of what they did. If they consider it a minor issue, then they will forgive them, but if it is, for example, murder, then revenge is all they have on their mind.

When Jesus was here on earth, he displayed lots of examples of forgiveness, especially with his disciples. So, what does that mean for us? If we are to duplicate Jesus, we must forgive as well on all levels. God will handle any repayment for injustices done to you. Remember, forgiveness is not for the person who hurt you, it is for you so you can live your life free from bitterness, anger, and revenge.

Chapter 4
Patience

The Prodigal Sons Father–He Waited

So, we have reached the halfway point of this book and if you have had none of the previous topics hit home yet, I'm confident this one will. If you are one of the select few that don't have an issue with patience, I commend you. You know how they say that 98% of the people are living in survival mode or below and 2% are above well those numbers also apply to people regarding having patience. Most people don't like to wait for anything, and I am one of them. Yes, I can admit my weaknesses. However, God has been working on me and it has gotten much better.

Patience means the capacity, habit, or fact of being patient, being able to remain calm and not become annoyed when waiting for a long time or when dealing with problems or troublesome people; done carefully over a long period without hurrying. .

We have become a fast-paced society. We have no patience or time for anything! Once electricity was created, the world was on the move. We could cook food in ovens and stoves, but that was not fast enough, so the microwave was invented. Did you know that in foreign countries like Italy, they prefer not to use microwaves? Italians in Italy have a different pace of life than Americans in America. They are not in such a big hurry that they force their meals into tiny microseconds. They enjoy eating. The act of coming together to enjoy a meal is very important to them. We had dial up internet and that became obsolete with lightning high speed internet.

Think about how complex the human body and life on earth are. We have cells, organs, organ systems, homeostasis mechanisms, a highly functional brain... these things and more. They are so complex and so many building blocks are required for them to function, yet they do. Even GOD took six days to create the earth. And God saw everything that he had made and, behold, it was very good. And the evening and the morning were the sixth day. - Genesis 1:31- KJV.

We must learn to endure and be patient! Not everything can be at lightning speed:

A mother carries a child for nine months unless it is premature

The children of Israel had to endure 40 years in the wilderness

A farmer must be patient when he plants his seeds waiting for a harvest

If you are caught speeding, endure and wait patiently for the officer to either give you a warning and let you go or even longer if he writes you a ticket.

QUOTES ON PATIENCE

"He that can have patience can have what he will." —— Benjamin Franklin

"Patience is bitter, but its fruit is sweet." —— Aristotle

"Toleration is the greatest gift of the mind; it requires the same effort of the brain that it takes to balance oneself on a bicycle." —— Helen Keller

"It is easier to find men who will volunteer to die, than to find those who are willing to endure pain with patience." - Julius Caesar

"Patience serves as a protection against wrongs as clothes do against cold. For if you put on more clothes as the cold increases, it will have no power to hurt you.

So, in like manner you must grow in patience when you meet with great wrongs, and they will then be powerless to vex your mind" - Leonardo da Vinci.

The Prodigal Sons Father had a great deal of patience with his son, waiting for him to return home after he asked his father for his portion of money and then went and squandered it all on foolish things.

Luke 15:11-22

King James Version

And he said, a certain man had two sons: and the younger of them said to his father, Father, give me the portion of goods that falleth to me. And he divided unto them his living. And not many days after, the younger son gathered all together, and took his journey into a far country, and there wasted his substance with riotous living. And when he had spent all, there arose a mighty famine in that land; and he began to be in want. And he went and joined himself to a citizen of that country; and he sent him into his fields to feed swine. And he would fain have filled his belly with the husks that the swine did eat, and no man gave unto him. And when he came to himself, he said, how many hired servants of my fathers have bread enough and to spare, and I perish with hunger! I will arise and go to my father, and will say unto him, Father, I have sinned against heaven, and before thee, and am no more worthy to be called thy son: make me as one of thy hired servants. And he arose and came to his father. But when he was yet a great way off, his father saw him, and had compassion, and ran, and fell on his neck, and kissed him. And the son said unto him, Father, I have sinned against heaven, and in thy sight, and am no more worthy to be called thy son. But the father said to his servants, "Bring forth the best robe, and put it on him; and put a ring on his hand, and shoes on his feet "

This story can cover a vast number of areas such as love, forgiveness, joy, gratitude, but we are zoning in on the patience factor that this father had in waiting and, of course, praying for his son's return.

The word patience is listed in the Bible almost 70 times. Apparently, God was very serious about us gaining and striving to be patient children of his. So much so that he included it in what he calls "The Fruit of the Spirit."

Galatians 5:22-23

Amplified Bible, Classic Edition

But the fruit of the [Holy] Spirit [the work which His presence within accomplishes] is love, joy (gladness), peace, patience (an even temper, forbearance), kindness, goodness (benevolence), faithfulness, gentleness (meekness, humility), self-control (self-restraint, continence). Against such things, there is no law that can bring a charge.

I have included some Bible verses on patience that you can read and commit to memory to help you if you struggle in this area.

And let us not be weary in well doing, for in due season we shall reap, if we faint not. - Galatians 6:9. KJV.

But those who wait for the Lord [who expect, look for, and hope in Him] shall change and renew their strength and power; they shall lift their wings and mount up [close to God] as eagles [mount up to the sun]; they shall run and not be weary, they shall walk and not faint or become tired. - Isaiah 40:31. – AMPC.

Rest in the LORD and wait patiently for him: fret not thyself because of him who prospereth in his way, because of the man who bringeth wicked devices to pass. - Psalm 37:7. – KJV.

Chapter 5
Gratitude

The only leper who returned to Jesus to give thanks

In everything give thanks: for this is the will of God in Christ Jesus concerning you. - 1 Thessalonians 5:18. – KJV.

"Do not spoil what you have by desiring what you have not; remember that what you now have was once among the things you only hoped for." - Epicurus.

"Gratitude makes sense of our past, brings peace for today, and creates a vision for tomorrow." - Melody Beattie

"Gratitude is the healthiest of all human emotions. The more you express gratitude for what you have, the more likely you will have even more to express gratitude for." - Zig Ziglar.

"It is through gratitude for the present moment that the spiritual dimension of life opens up." - Eckhart Tolle

What are you grateful for? Big things, small things, anything at all? "As in water face answers to and reflects face, so the heart of man to man."–Proverbs 27:19. – AMPC.

Rhonda Byrne, the bestselling author of the book "The Secret," that sold over 35 million copies worldwide, says this about gratitude, "Remember, if you are criticizing, you are not being grateful. If you are blaming, you are not being grateful. If you are complaining, you are not being grateful."

We have so much to be grateful for in life. It should be a simple thing when you wake up in the morning to name 10 things you are grateful for. The breath of life, food to eat, water to drink, any amount of mobility in your body, use of your five senses (they say that when one is not operating the others are enhanced), freedom of speech (especially if you live in the United States), transportation (even if you don't have a car–there is public transportation or bikes you can rent), your pets (they help you stay stress free and keep your blood pressure in check–not to mention all the times they make you laugh with their antics and quirky things they do and we all know laughter is the best medicine and completely free), I know some of you will not agree with this next one but pain (you have learned some lessons from pain and hopefully you will not repeat the same mistakes again, technology (everyone has some type of device nowadays even if they have hit hard times and are homeless. I was coming from an event the other night and it pained my heart to see so many homeless people on the streets, but this one man actually had a laptop and found an electrical outlet and was watching tv laying right there on the streets.)

If you think you have nothing to be grateful for, you are sorely mistaken. Every day take a pen and paper and write ten things to be grateful for and as you continue to do this, you will find you have even more to be grateful for and your list will enlarge.

Luke 17:11-19

Amplified Bible, Classic Edition

As He went on His way to Jerusalem, it occurred that [Jesus] was passing [along the border] between Samaria and Galilee. And as He was going into one village, He was met by ten lepers, who stood at a distance. And they raised up their voices and called, Jesus, Master, take pity and have mercy on us! And when He saw them, He said to them, Go [at once] and show yourselves to the priests. And as they went, they were cured and made clean. Then one of them, upon seeing that he was cured, turned back, recognizing and thanking and praising God with a loud voice and he fell prostrate at Jesus' feet thanking Him [over and over]. And he was a Samaritan. Then Jesus asked, Were not all ten cleansed? Where are the nine? Was there no one found to return and to recognize and give thanks and praise to God except this alien? And He said to him, Get up and go on your way. Your faith (your trust and confidence that spring from your belief in God) has restored you to health.

As you can tell, even Jesus was astonished at the lack of gratitude that was given to him for healing 10 lepers and only one came back to give thanks. Having gratitude and showing it will catapult your life faster than anything else.

"Often people ask how I manage to be happy despite having no arms and no legs. The quick answer is that I have a choice. I can be angry about not having limbs, or I can be thankful that I have a purpose. I chose gratitude." - Nick Vujicic

Chapter 6
Peace

Abigail–Nabal's Wife – The Peacemaker

"Deceit is in the hearts of those who plot evil, but those who promote peace have joy. –Proverbs 12:20 CSB

"When a person's ways please the Lord, he makes even his enemies to be at peace with him."–Proverbs 16:7 CSB

The story of Nabal and his wife Abigail is very poignant. They say that most couples are opposites of each other, and, in this case, it was right on point. Nabal was a very wealthy man, but also a very pompous man. His wife, Abigail, however, was a woman of intelligence and beauty. Now before David became king, he sent men to ask Nabal for provisions and Nabal was curse and rude and so David gathered a large army of his men to destroy Nabal. However, one of his men notified Abigail, and she went to David to give him the provisions and keep the peace. Let's look at the story.

1 Samuel 25

King James Version

And Samuel died; and all the Israelites were gathered together, and lamented him, and buried him in his house at Ramah. And David arose and went down to the wilderness of Paran. And there was a man in Maon, whose possessions were in Carmel — and the man was very great, and he had three thousand sheep, and a thousand goats: and he was shearing his sheep in Carmel. Now the name of the man was Nabal; and the name of his wife Abigail: and she was a woman of good understanding, and of a beautiful countenance: but the man was churlish and evil in his doings; and he was of the house of Caleb.

And David heard in the wilderness that Nabal did shear his sheep. And David sent out ten young men, and David said unto the young men, Get you up to Carmel, and go to Nabal, and greet him in my name: And thus, shall ye say to him that liveth in prosperity, Peace be both to thee, and peace be to thine house, and peace be unto all that thou hast. And now I have heard that thou hast shearers: now thy shepherds which were with us, we hurt them not, neither was there ought missing unto them, all the while they were in Carmel. Ask thy young men, and they will shew thee. Wherefore let the young men find favour in thine eyes: for we come in a good day: give, I pray thee, whatsoever cometh to thine hand unto thy servants, and to thy son David. And when David's young men came, they spake to Nabal according to all those words in the name of David and ceased. And Nabal answered David's servants, and said, "Who is David? And who is the son of Jesse? There be many servants now a days that break away every man from his master. Shall I then take my bread, and my water, and my flesh that I have killed for my shearers, and give it unto men, whom I know not whence they be? So, David's young men turned their way, and went again, and came and told him all those sayings. And David said unto his men, Gird ye on every man his sword. And they girded on every man his sword; and David also girded on his sword: and there went up after David about four hundred men; and two hundred abode by the stuff. But one of the young men told Abigail, Nabal's wife, saying, Behold, David sent messengers out of the wilderness to salute our master; and he railed on them. But the men were very good unto us, and we were not hurt, neither missed we anything, as long as we were conversant with them, when we were in the fields: They were a wall unto us both by night and day, all the while we were with them keeping the sheep. Now therefore know and consider what thou wilt do; for evil is determined against our master, and against all his household: for he is such a son of Belial, that a man cannot speak to him. Then Abigail made haste, and took two hundred loaves, and two bottles of wine, and five sheep ready dressed, and five measures of parched corn, and an hundred clusters of raisins, and two hundred cakes of figs, and laid them on asses. And she said unto her servants, Go on before me; behold, I come after you. But she told not her husband Nabal. And it was so, as she rode on the ass, that she came down by the covert on the hill, and behold, David and his men came down against her; and she met them. Now David had said, Surely in vain have I kept all that this fellow hath in the wilderness, so that nothing was missed of all that pertained unto him: and he hath requited me evil for good. So, and more also do God unto the enemies of David, if I leave of all that pertain to him by the morning light, any that pisseth against the wall. And when Abigail saw David, she hasted, and lighted off the ass, and fell before David on her face, and bowed herself to the ground, And fell at his feet, and said, Upon me, my lord, upon me let this iniquity be: and let thine handmaid, I pray thee, speak in thine audience, and hear the words of thine handmaid. Let not my lord, I pray thee, regard this man of Belial, even Nabal: for as his name is, so is he; Nabal is his name, and folly is with him: but I thine handmaid saw not the young men of my lord, whom thou didst send. Now therefore, my lord, as the Lord liveth, and as thy soul liveth, seeing the Lord hath withholden thee from coming to shed blood, and from avenging thyself with thine own hand, now let thine enemies, and they that seek evil to my lord, be as Nabal. And now this blessing which thine handmaid hath brought unto my lord, let it even be given unto the young men that follow my lord. I pray thee, forgive the trespass of thine handmaid: for the Lord will certainly make my lord a sure house; because my lord fighteth the battles of the Lord, and evil hath not been found in thee all thy days. Yet a man is risen to pursue thee, and to seek thy soul: but the soul of my lord shall be bound in the bundle of life with the Lord thy God; and the souls of thine enemies, them shall he sling out, as out of the middle of a sling. And it shall come to pass, when the Lord shall have done to my lord according to all the good that he hath spoken concerning thee, and shall have appointed thee ruler over Israel; That this shall be no grief unto thee, nor offence of heart unto my lord, either that thou hast shed blood causeless, or that my lord hath avenged himself: but when the Lord shall have dealt well with my lord, then remember thine handmaid. And David said to Abigail, Blessed be the Lord God of Israel, which sent thee this day to meet me: And blessed be thy advice, and blessed be thou, which hast kept me this day from coming to shed blood, and from avenging myself with mine own hand. For in very deed, as the Lord God of Israel liveth, which hath kept me back from hurting thee, except thou hadst hasted and come to meet me, surely there had not been left unto Nabal by the morning light any that pisseth against the wall. So, David received of her hand that which she had brought him, and said unto her, Go up in peace to thine house; see, I have hearkened to thy voice, and have accepted thy person. And Abigail came to Nabal; and behold, he held a feast in his house, like the feast of a king; and Nabal's heart was merry within him, for he was very drunken: wherefore she told him nothing, less or more, until the morning light. But it came to pass in the morning, when the wine was gone out of Nabal, and his wife had told him these things, that his heart died within him, and he became as a stone. And it came to pass about ten days after, that the Lord smote Nabal, that he died. And when David heard that Nabal was dead, he said, Blessed be the Lord, that hath pleaded the cause of my reproach from the hand of Nabal, and hath kept his servant from evil: for the Lord hath returned the wickedness of Nabal upon his own head. And David sent and communed with Abigail, to take her to him to wife. And when the servants of David were come to Abigail to Carmel, they spake unto her, saying, David sent us unto thee, to take thee to him to wife. And she arose, and bowed herself on her face to the earth, and said, Behold, let thine handmaid be a servant to wash the feet of the servants of my lord. And Abigail hasted, and arose and rode upon an ass, with five damsels of hers that went after her; and she went after the messengers of David and became his wife.

The first thing I want you all to see is that God took his revenge on Nabal and killed him. We previously discussed in chapter 2 about forgiveness why we should not take revenge on people who do us wrong, because God says he will repay. So, what can we do on a daily spiritual basis to instill peace? Let us look at an acronym I wrote for peace and start there.

P = Profess - Everyone of us has had a godly experience of some sort that we know human flesh was incapable of making that situation even happen or happen as swiftly as it did. In my situation, it was to quit smoking instantly after over 27 years or more of smoking every day with no patches, smokeless cigarettes, or anything at all. Now that was a miracle, and I have never gone back. Whatever your experience is, profess it to the world what God has done for you.

E = Educate - Talk and teach others about how wonderful it is to be a child of God. For God so loved the world, that he gave his only begotten Son, that whosoever believeth in him should not perish, but have everlasting life. - John 3:16. – KJV. He that spared not his own Son, but delivered him up for us all, how shall he not with him also freely give us all things? - Romans 8:32. – KJV.

A = Appreciate - We all need to show gratitude to God for all that he has done for us daily. We have all heard the phrase " the little things mean so much", well that is true. Be grateful for things you never think about. Are you able to walk, talk, drive, see, hear, go to the bathroom by yourself without the help of a wheelchair or human being? If so, then you are already out of the starting gate doing well and we all know how that turned out for "Justify" (the racing world's latest triple crown winner in 2018).

C = Charity - In our world nowadays, there are multitudes of companies asking for charity. However, you must be selective about who you choose to help, but you are required by God to assist. For ye have the poor always with you; but me ye have not always. - Matthew 26:11. – KJV. A good man sheweth favour, and lendeth: he will guide his affairs with discretion. Surely, he shall not be moved forever: the righteous shall be in everlasting remembrance. He shall not be afraid of evil tidings: his heart is fixed, trusting in the Lord. His heart is established, he shall not be afraid, until he see his desire upon his enemies. He hath dispersed, he hath given to the poor; his righteousness endureth for ever; his horn shall be exalted with honour. - Psalms 112: 5-9. KJV.

E = Empathy - We have all also heard the phrase "walk a mile in my shoes" but would we really want to in some circumstances? There is a reason God gave us two ears and one mouth so we can listen and share other people's feelings, experiences, and emotions. "Before you criticize someone, you should walk a mile in their shoes. That way when you criticize them, you are a mile away from them and you have their shoes." - Jack Handey.

I hope and pray that I have been able to show you the importance of always living peacefully with your fellow man. Sometimes we can be so wasteful with the food that God has provided for us and there are so many starving people all over the world but let's try not to be wasteful with a quote from the great civil rights leader Dr. Martin Luther King Jr., "We must come to see that the end we seek is a society at peace with itself, a society that can live with its conscience."

Chapter 7
Love

Jesus - He Gave His Life In The Name Of Love

John 13:34-35

King James Version

A new commandment I give unto you, That ye love one another; as I have loved you, that ye also love one another. By this shall all men know that ye are my disciples, if ye have love one to another.

1 John 4:8

Amplified Bible, Classic Edition

He who does not love has not become acquainted with God [does not and never did know Him], for God is love.

Jesus is our benchmark for love! The way Jesus expects us to love is exactly the way he lived his earthly life. Let's look at some ways Jesus loves, i.e. compassion, respect, listening, and encouraging.

Jesus is the epitome of compassion, and he reflected that while he was here on earth and continues to do the same up in heaven, seated on the right hand of the father.

Jesus wept before he raised Lazarus from the dead: "When the Jews who were sitting with her in the house and consoling her saw how hastily Mary had arisen and gone out, they followed her, supposing that she was going to the tomb to pour out her grief there. When Mary came to the place where Jesus was and saw Him, she dropped down at His feet, saying to Him, Lord, if You had been here, my brother would not have died. When Jesus saw her sobbing, and the Jews who came with her [also] sobbing, He was deeply moved in spirit and troubled. [He chafed in spirit and sighed and was disturbed.] And He said, Where have you laid him? They said to Him, Lord, come and see. Jesus wept."–John 11:31-35. – AMPC

Jesus feeding 5,000 people: "When Jesus heard it, He withdrew from there privately in a boat to a solitary place. But when the crowds heard of it, they followed Him [by land] on foot from the towns. When He went ashore and saw a great throng of people, He had compassion (pity and deep sympathy) for them and cured their sick. When evening came, the disciples came to Him and said, This is a remote and barren place, and the day is now over; send the throngs away into the villages to buy food for themselves. Jesus said, They do not need to go away; you give them something to eat. They said to Him, "We have nothing here but five loaves and two fish. He said, "Bring them here to Me. Then He ordered the crowds to recline on the grass; and He took the five loaves and the two fish, and, looking up to heaven, He gave thanks and blessed and broke the loaves and handed the pieces to the disciples, and the disciples gave them to the people. And they all ate and were satisfied. And they picked up twelve [small hand] baskets full of the broken pieces left over. And those who ate were about 5,000 men, not including women and children."–Matthew 14:13-21. - AMPC. Jesus also fed 4,000 which is reflected in the book of Matthew 15:32-39.

Jesus forgiving lost people: "For the Son of Man came to seek and to save that which was lost."–Luke 19:10. – AMPC

The woman with the issue of blood: "And there was a woman who had had a flow of blood for twelve years, And who had endured much suffering under [the hands of] many physicians and had spent all that she had and was no better but instead grew worse. She had heard the reports concerning Jesus, and she came up behind Him in the throng and touched His garment, For she kept saying, If I only touch His garments, I shall be restored to health. And immediately her flow of blood was dried up at the source, and [suddenly] she felt in her body that she was healed of her [distressing] ailment. And Jesus, recognizing in Himself that the power proceeding from Him had gone forth, turned around immediately in the crowd and said, Who touched My clothes? And the disciples kept saying to Him, You see the crowd pressing hard around You from all sides, and You ask, Who touched Me? Still, He kept looking around to see her who had done it. But the woman, knowing what had been done for her, though alarmed and frightened and trembling, fell before Him and told Him the whole truth. And He said to her, Daughter, your faith (your trust and confidence in Me, springing from faith in God) has restored you to health. Go in (into) peace and be continually healed and freed from your [distressing bodily] disease."–Mark 5:25-34. - AMPC.

The paralyzed man: "And Jesus having returned to Capernaum, after some days it was rumored about that He was in the house [probably Peter's]. And so many people gathered together there that there was no longer room [for them], not even around the door; and He was discussing the Word. Then they came, bringing a paralytic to Him, who had been picked up and was being carried by four men. And when they could not get him to a place in front of Jesus because of the throng, they dug through the roof above Him; and when they had scooped out an opening, they let down the [thickly padded] quilt or mat upon which the paralyzed man lay. And when Jesus saw their faith [their confidence in God through Him], He said to the paralyzed man, Son, your sins are forgiven [you] and put away [that is, the penalty is remitted, the sense of guilt removed, and you are made upright and in right standing with God]. Now some of the scribes were sitting there, holding a dialogue with themselves as they questioned in their hearts, Why does this man talk like this? He is blaspheming! Who can forgive sins [remove guilt, remit the penalty, and bestow righteousness instead] except God alone? And at once Jesus, becoming fully aware in His spirit that they thus debated within themselves, said to them, Why do you argue (debate, reason) about all this in your hearts? Which is easier: to say to the paralyzed man, Your sins are forgiven and [put away, or to say, Rise, take up your sleeping pad or mat, and start walking about [and keep on walking]? But that you may know positively and beyond a doubt that the Son of Man has right and authority and power on earth to forgive sins—He said to the paralyzed man, I say to you, arise, pick up and carry your sleeping pad or mat, and be going on home. And he arose at once and picked up the sleeping pad or mat and went out before them all, so that they were all amazed and recognized and praised and thanked God, saying, We have never seen anything like this before! –Mark 2:1-12. - AMPC.

Jesus respected everyone; he was no respecter of persons. "For God shows no partiality [undue favor or unfairness; with Him, one man is not different from another]. –Romans 2:11. - AMPC.

Jesus respected and held women in high esteem. "Now Simon's mother-in-law had for some time been lying sick with a fever, and at once they told Him about her. And He went up to her and took her by the hand and raised her up; and the fever left her, and she began to wait on them."–Mark 1:30-31. - AMPC.

"Soon afterward, Jesus went to a town called Nain, and His disciples and a great throng accompanied Him. [Just] as He drew near the gate of the town, behold, a man who had died was being carried out—the only son of his mother, and she was a widow; and a large gathering from the town was accompanying her. When the Lord saw her, He had compassion on her and said to her, Do not weep. And He went forward and touched the funeral bier, and the pallbearers stood still. And He said, Young man, I say to you, arise [death]! And the man [who was] dead sat up and began to speak. And [Jesus] gave him [back] to his mother. –Luke 7:11-15. - AMPC.

"Now Jesus was teaching in one of the synagogues on the Sabbath. And there was a woman there who, for eighteen years, had had an infirmity caused by a spirit (a demon of sickness). She was bent completely forward and utterly unable to straighten herself up or to look upward. And when Jesus saw her, He called [her to Him] and said to her, Woman, you are released from your infirmity! Then He laid [His] hands on her, and instantly she was made straight, and she recognized and thanked and praised God. But the leader of the synagogue, indignant because Jesus had healed on the Sabbath, said to the crowd, There are six days on which work ought to be done; so, come on those days and be cured, and not on the Sabbath day. But the Lord replied to him, saying, You playactors (hypocrites)! Does not each one of you on the Sabbath loose his ox or his donkey from the stall and lead it out to water it? And ought not this woman, a daughter of Abraham, whom Satan has kept bound for eighteen years, be loosed from this bond on the Sabbath day? Even as He said this, all His opponents were put to shame, and all the people were rejoicing over all the glorious things that were being done by Him. –Luke 13:10-17. - AMPC.

Jesus respected and loved children.

And they kept bringing young children to Him that He might touch them, and the disciples were reproving them [for it]. But when Jesus saw [it], He was indignant and pained and said to them, Allow the children to come to Me—do not forbid or prevent or hinder them—for to such belongs the kingdom of God. Truly I tell you, whoever does not receive and accept and welcome the kingdom of God like a little child [does] positively shall not enter it at all. And He took them [the children up [one by one] in His arms and [fervently invoked a] blessing, placing His hands upon them. –Mark 10:13-16. - AMPC.

Jesus respected the poor: "For you always have the poor among you, but you will not always have Me."–Matthew 26:11. - AMPC.

"The Spirit of the Lord [is] upon Me, because He has anointed Me [the Anointed One, the Messiah] to preach the good news (the Gospel) to the poor; He has sent Me to announce release to the captives and recovery of sight to the blind, to send forth as delivered those who are oppressed [who are downtrodden, bruised, crushed, and broken down by calamity], To proclaim the accepted and acceptable year of the Lord [the day when salvation and the free favors of God profusely abound].–Luke 4:18-19. - AMPC.

Jesus was an excellent listener.

Jesus listened to a Samaritan woman: "It was necessary for Him to go through Samaria. And in doing so, He arrived at a Samaritan town called Sychar, near the tract of land that Jacob gave to his son Joseph. And Jacob's well was there. So, Jesus, tired as He was from His journey, sat down [to rest] by the well. It was then about the sixth hour (about noon). Presently, when a woman of Samaria came along to draw water, Jesus said to her, Give Me a drink—For His disciples had gone off into the town to buy food— Samaritan woman said to Him, How is it that You, being a Jew, ask me, a Samaritan [and a] woman, for a drink?—For the Jews have nothing to do with the Samaritans, answered her, If you had only known and had recognized God's gift and Who this is that is saying to you, Give Me a drink, you would have asked Him [instead] and He would have given you living water. Said to Him, Sir, You have nothing to draw with [no drawing bucket] and the well is deep; how then can you provide living water? [Where do You get Your living water?] Are You greater than and superior to our ancestor Jacob, who gave us this well and who used to drink from it himself, and his sons and his cattle also? Jesus answered her, All who drink of this water will be thirsty again. But whoever takes a drink of the water that I will give him shall never, no never, be thirsty anymore. But the water that I will give him shall become a spring of water welling up (flowing, bubbling) [continually] within him unto (into, for) eternal life. The woman said to Him, Sir, give me this water, so that I may never get thirsty nor have to come [continually all the way] here to draw. This, Jesus said to her, Go, call your husband and come back here. The woman answered, I have no husband. Jesus said to her, You have spoken truly in saying, I have no husband. For you have had five husbands, and the man you are now living with is not your husband. In this, you have spoken truly. The woman said to Him, Sir, I see and understand that You are a prophet. Our forefathers worshiped on this mountain, but you [Jews] say that Jerusalem is the place where it is necessary and proper to worship. Jesus said to her, Woman, believe Me, a time is coming when you will worship the Father neither [merely] in this mountain nor [merely] in Jerusalem. You [Samaritans] do not know what you are worshiping [you worship what you do not comprehend]. We do know what we are worshiping [we worship what we have knowledge of and understand], for [after all] salvation comes from [among] the Jews. A time will come, however, indeed it is already here, when the true (genuine) worshipers will worship the Father in spirit and in truth (reality); for the Father is seeking just such people as these as His worshipers. God is a Spirit (a spiritual Being) and those who worship Him must worship Him in spirit and in truth (reality). The woman said to Him, I know that Messiah is coming, He Who is called the Christ (the Anointed One); and when He arrives, He will tell us everything we need to know and make it clear to us. Jesus said to her, I Who now speak with you am He. Just then, His disciples came, and they wondered (were surprised, astonished) to find Him talking with a woman [a married woman]. However, not one of them asked Him, What are You inquiring about? or what do you want? Or, why do you speak with her? Then the woman left her water jar and went away to the town. And she began telling the people, Come, see a Man Who has told me everything that I ever did! Can this be [is not this] the Christ? [Must not this be the Messiah, the Anointed One?] So, the people left the town and set out to go to Him. –John 4:4-30. - AMPC.

Jesus was a devout encourager:

Jesus encouraged his disciples: "I assure you, most solemnly I tell you, if anyone steadfastly believes in Me, he will himself be able to do the things that I do; and he will do even greater things than these, because I go to the Father." - John 14:12. - AMPC.

Jesus encouraged the paralytic: "And behold, they brought to Him a man paralyzed and prostrated by illness, lying on a sleeping pad; and when Jesus saw their faith, He said to the paralyzed man, Take courage, son; your sins are forgiven, and the penalty remitted." – Matthew 9:2. - AMPC.

Jesus encouraged the woman that was hemorrhaging: "Jesus turned around and, seeing her, He said, Take courage, daughter! Your faith has made you well. And at once the woman was restored to health." – Matthew 9:22. - AMPC.

So, as we can see, Jesus showed love in many ways and on many levels and is still doing so presently. Let's look at an acronym for love that Jesus displayed here on earth and is still pouring out upon us all today.

L = Love

"The infinity of God is that perfection of God by which he is free from all limitations." - Louis Berkhof

"Yours, O Lord, is the greatness and the power and the glory and the victory and the majesty, for all that is in the heavens and the earth is yours; yours is the kingdom, O Lord, and Yours it is to be exalted as Head overall."–1 Chronicles 29:11. - AMPC.

God's love for us is limitless. That is why he gave us power and dominion over the entire earth.

"O lord, thou hast searched me, and known me. Thou knowest my downsitting and mine uprising, thou understandest my thought afar off. Thou compassest my path and my lying down, and art acquainted with all my ways. For there is not a word in my tongue, but, lo, O Lord, thou knowest it altogether. Thou hast beset me behind and before and laid thine hand upon me. Such knowledge is too wonderful for me; it is high, I cannot attain unto it. Whither shall I go from thy spirit? Or whither shall I flee from thy presence? If I ascend up into heaven, thou art there: if I make my bed in hell, behold, thou art there. If I take the wings of the morning, and dwell in the uttermost parts of the sea; Even there shall thy hand lead me, and thy right hand shall hold me. If I say, Surely the darkness shall cover me; even the night shall be light about me. Yea, the darkness hideth not from thee; but the night shineth as the day: the darkness and the light are both alike to thee. –Psalms 139:1-12. - KJV.

"And God said, Let us make man in our image, after our likeness: and let them have dominion over the fish of the sea, and over the fowl of the air, and over the cattle, and over all the earth, and over every creeping thing that creepeth upon the earth. So, God created man in his own image, in the image of God created he him; male and female created he them. And God blessed them, and God said unto them, Be fruitful, and multiply, and replenish the earth, and subdue it: and have dominion over the fish of the sea, and over the fowl of the air, and over every living thing that moveth upon the earth. –Genesis 1:26-28. - KJV.

O = Overflowing

One name for God is El Shaddai, which means "the God of plenty" or "the All-Sufficient One". This was displayed many times in the Bible; however, we will look at the manna God provided for the children of Israel for the 40 years they were traveling to get to the promise land.

And they took their journey from Elim, and all the congregation of the children of Israel came unto the wilderness of Sin, which is between Elim and Sinai, on the fifteenth day of the second month after their departing out of the land of Egypt. And the whole congregation of the children of Israel murmured against Moses and Aaron in the wilderness, and the children of Israel said unto them, Would to God we had died by the hand of the Lord in the land of Egypt, when we sat by the fleshpots, and when we did eat bread to the full; for ye have brought us forth into this wilderness, to kill this whole assembly with hunger. Then said the Lord unto Moses, Behold, I will rain bread from heaven for you; and the people shall go out and gather a certain rate every day, that I may prove them, whether they will walk in my law, or no. And it shall come to pass that on the sixth day they shall prepare that which they bring in; and it shall be twice as much as they gather daily. And Moses and Aaron said unto all the children of Israel, At even, then ye shall know that the Lord hath brought you out from the land of Egypt: And in the morning, then ye shall see the glory of the Lord; for that he heareth your murmurings against the Lord: and what are we, that ye murmur against us? And Moses said, This shall be when the Lord shall give you in the evening flesh to eat, and in the morning bread to the full; for that the Lord heareth your murmurings which ye murmur against him: and what are we? Your murmurings are not against us, but against the Lord. And Moses spake unto Aaron, Say unto all the congregation of the children of Israel, Come near before the Lord: for he hath heard your murmurings. And it came to pass, as Aaron spake unto the whole congregation of the children of Israel, that they looked toward the wilderness, and behold, the glory of the Lord appeared in the cloud. And the Lord spake unto Moses, saying, I have heard the murmurings of the children of Israel: speak unto them, saying, At even ye shall eat flesh, and in the morning ye shall be filled with bread; and ye shall know that I am the Lord your God. And it came to pass, that at even the quails came up, and covered the camp: and in the morning the dew lay round about the host. And when the dew that lay was gone up, behold, upon the face of the wilderness there lay a small round thing, as small as the hoar frost on the ground. And when the children of Israel saw it, they said one to another; It is manna: for they wist not what it was. And Moses said unto them, This is the bread which the Lord hath given you to eat. This is the thing which the Lord hath commanded, Gather of it every man according to his eating, an omer for every man, according to the number of your persons; take ye every man for them which are in his tents. And the children of Israel did so, and gathered, some more, some less. And when they did mete it with an omer, he that gathered much had nothing over, and he that gathered little had no lack; they gathered every man according to his eating. And Moses said, Let no man leave of it till the morning. Notwithstanding, they hearkened not unto Moses; but some of them left of it until the morning, and it bred worms, and stank and Moses was wroth with them. And they gathered it every morning, every man according to his eating: and when the sun waxed hot, it melted. And it came to pass that on the sixth day they gathered twice as much bread, two omers for one man: and all the rulers of the congregation came and told Moses. And he said unto them, This is that which the Lord hath said, tomorrow is the rest of the holy sabbath unto the Lord: bake that which ye will bake to day, and seethe that ye will seethe; and that which remaineth over lay up for you to be kept until the morning. And they laid it up till the morning, as Moses bade and it did not stink, neither was there any worm therein. And Moses said, Eat that today; for today is a sabbath unto the Lord: today ye shall not find it in the field. Six days ye shall gather it; but on the seventh day, which is the sabbath, in it there shall be none. And it came to pass, that there went out some of the people on the seventh day for to gather, and they found none. And the Lord said unto Moses, How long refuse ye to keep my commandments and my laws? See, for that the Lord hath given you the sabbath, therefore he giveth you on the sixth day the bread of two days; abide ye every man in his place, let no man go out of his place on the seventh day. So, the people rested on the seventh day. And the house of Israel called the name thereof Manna: and it was like coriander seed, white; and the taste of it was like wafers made with honey. And Moses said, This is the thing which the Lord commandeth, Fill an omer of it to be kept for your generations; that they may see the bread wherewith I have fed you in the wilderness, when I brought you forth from the land of Egypt. And Moses said unto Aaron, Take a pot, and put an omer full of manna therein, and lay it up before the Lord, to be kept for your generations. the Lord commanded Moses, so Aaron laid it up before the Testimony, to be kept. And the children of Israel did eat manna for forty years until they came to a land inhabited; they did eat manna until they came unto the borders of the land of Canaan. Now an omer is the tenth part of an ephah. - Exodus 16. - KJV.

V = Virtues

In the Bible, it states that virtues that are linked with holiness and our mental pictures, along with taking steps to bond with God we should meditate on. There are a total of seven virtues. There are the cardinal virtues, which are prudence, temperance, fortitude, and justice. There are also the theological virtues, which are faith, hope, and love. However, we are more familiar with the virtues that the apostle Paul called "The Fruit of the Spirit" which are: love, joy, peace, longsuffering, gentleness, goodness, faith. "Finally, brethren, whatsoever things are true, whatsoever things are honest, whatsoever things are just, whatsoever things are pure, whatsoever things are lovely, whatsoever things are of good report; if there be any virtue, and if there be any praise, think on these things." - Philippians 4:8. - KJV.

E = Everlasting

"Before the mountains were brought forth, or ever thou hadst formed the earth and the world, even from everlasting to everlasting, thou art God." - Psalms 90:2. - KJV.

"But the mercy of the Lord is from everlasting to everlasting upon them that fear him, and his righteousness unto children's children."–Psalms 103:17. - KJV.

"Hast thou not known? hast thou not heard that the everlasting God, the Lord, the Creator of the ends of the earth, fainteth not, neither is weary? There is no searching of his understanding. He giveth power to the faint; and to them that have no might, he increaseth strength. Even the youths shall faint and be weary, and the young men shall utterly fall: But they that wait upon the Lord shall renew their strength; they shall mount up with wings as eagles; they shall run and not be weary; and they shall walk and not faint." - Isaiah 40:28-31. - KJV.

It is time to Let go and Let God. He is Alpha and Omega, and he is in total control. If you will just believe, have faith, and trust in him he will guide your every step and give you the great life he had planned for you even before he formed you in your mother's womb to navigate living in this fallen world with empowerment and encouragement.

Chapter 8
Empowerment Quotes

We need to see examples of empowerment, because when we see that... it seems like that's the norm. - Lindsey Morgan

Confidence and empowerment are cousins, in my opinion. Empowerment comes from within and typically it's stemmed and fostered by self-assurance. To feel empowered is to feel free, and that's when people do their best work. You can't fake confidence or empowerment. - Amy Jo Martin

Empowerment is not about doing the same thing the same way in the same environment. It's about building the man and the woman and doing so with a view to creating better citizens and, by extension, better patriots in this society of ours. - Anthony Carmona

Ultimately, so much Dr. Seuss is about empowerment. He invites us to disappear into our imagination and then blows the doors off what that can mean. –Gary Ross.

ENCOURAGEMENT QUOTES

When you encourage others, you, in the process, are encouraged because you're making a commitment and difference in that person's life. Encouragement really does make a difference. - Zig Ziglar

A word of encouragement from a teacher to a child can change a life. A word of encouragement from a spouse can save a marriage. A word of encouragement from a leader can inspire a person to reach her potential. –John C. Maxwell.

Instead of being critical of people in authority over you and envious of their position, be happy you're not responsible for everything they have to do. Instead of piling on complaints, thank them for what they do. Overwhelm them with encouragement and appreciation! –Joyce Meyer.

I don't give advice. 90% of the time nobody takes it anyway. I will give encouragement and if asked a question as to how, or why I did certain things and if I think this will help whomever is asking the question, I will do this. - Dionne Warwick

About the Author

Raised in New York, Donna has always had a penchant for writing. Constantly surrounded by pen and paper, Donna studied writing courses at Queensboro Community College in New York. The Institute of Children's Writers and Long Ridge Writers Group are in Connecticut. She moved to Florida and because of her relationship with The Holy Spirit; she wrote a book on miracles.

Donna's first book Miracles of Direction Miracles of Conquest Miracles of Provision Miracles of Purpose helped readers explore miracles, both past and present. The book explores biblical miracles that took place while Jesus was here on earth. She then references miracles that take place daily in the modern world. She separates these miracles into four categories and presents insightful examples of each type, taken directly from the Bible.

They chose her as the winner in the 2018 Top Female Author Awards in the Religion/Philosophy/Spiritual category from The Author Show. They chose Donna from an international field of contestants by a panel of judges. The Author Show also chose her as a winner in 50 Great Writers You Should Be Reading in 2015, 2016, 2017 and 2018.

Donna Louis' second book best-selling book, 'Thriving in Every Season of Life with God', gives us a road map to create a mindset - a new life in which we can learn to prosper in any circumstance, however dire. The book achieved bestseller status in two categories: Spiritual Self Help and Motivational Self Help. This book received a Five Star review from Readers Favorite.

Donna's third book best-selling book, "Book of Proverbs–Proverbs For The Modern Day" provides intellectual depth, insights, and exceptional wisdom on how to live a meaningful, joyful, and tranquil life by honoring and respecting God as omnipotent. The book achieved bestseller status in six categories: Christian Inspiration, Christian Devotionals, Christian Living, Religion & Spirituality, Christian E-Books & Bibles & Christian Spiritual Growth. This book received a Five Star review from Readers Favorite.

Donna's next book, The Rain Falls On The Just & The Unjust, achieved best-seller status in the following categories: Spiritual Growth Self-Help, Christian Prayer, & Christian Self-Help. This book received a Five Star review from Readers Favorite.

Donna Louis' last book Pearls Of Wisdom: Inspirational Motivational Bible Quotes For Challenging Situations. This book is a road map of how to handle challenging situations that arise in our lives. There are also prayers that you can read and say over these situations that will inspire you, bring you peace and bless your life incredibly. The book achieved bestseller status in the Christian Spiritual Growth category. As a Christian we should desire and crave wisdom more than anything as a directive in our daily lives. Desiring and asking God for wisdom daily will please God immensely. This alone will have him rain down showers of blessings on our lives.

This book will provide you with a plethora of motivational and inspirational quotes from some of the greatest people that ever lived. Some have traveled through their journey of life and many others still are and they have gifted us with some of the greatest thoughts, examples, and testimonies for life ever.

The greatest book ever created the Bible is also referenced with some thought-provoking guides on how we should carry ourselves and live our lives. We are constantly in thought, like the statue "The Thinker" about what we should do with our lives, how to live our lives, and the choices that we make are critical because they will determine our destiny. This is not something that we just want to flip a coin and see if it comes down heads or tails. We need to be grateful for the life God gave us and live it to his glory.

Donna has been married to her husband of 40 years Patrick Louis and lives in Florida. She lives to accomplish the task that God created her for and daily to follow Proverbs 3:5-6. "Trust in the Lord with all thine heart and lean not unto thine own understanding. In all thy ways acknowledge him, and he shall direct thy paths."

Acknowledgements

I want to acknowledge and thank three beautiful women of God who are my church sisters and my ladies' night out crew: Carmen, Nelly, and Natasha. You ladies have been there so often to encourage me and keep me lifted. May God continue to bless you all exceedingly and abundantly all of your lives. I love you all.

I also want to acknowledge my spiritual mentors, my D & D connection with Pastor Dave and Dave, my growth leader. You two have been a tremendous blessing in my life and elevating my spiritual growth, but also lots of fun to be around. God bless you both.

Other Books By Donna Louis

Pearls Of Wisdom: Inspirational Motivational Bible Quotes For Challenging Situations

As a Christian we should desire and crave wisdom more than anything as a directive in our daily lives. Desiring and asking God for wisdom daily will please God immensely. This alone will have him rain down showers of blessings on our lives.

This book will provide you with a plethora of motivational and inspirational quotes from some of the greatest people that ever lived. Some have traveled through their journey of life and many others still are and they have gifted us with some of the greatest thoughts, examples, and testimonies for life ever.

The greatest book ever created the Bible is also referenced with some thought-provoking guides on how we should carry ourselves and live our lives. We are constantly in thought, like the statue "The Thinker" about what we should do with our lives, how to live our lives, and the choices that we make are critical because they will determine our destiny. This is not something that we just want to flip a coin and see if it comes down heads or tails. We need to be grateful for the life God gave us and live it to his glory.

https://amzn.to/46DUKJt

Book Of Proverbs - Proverbs For The Modern Day

Best-Selling Author Donna Louis From The King James Version

Are you looking for inspiration?

This book can provide inspiration and motivation to help you overcome any challenge.

If you are struggling with daily life itself or maybe even deeper issues like suicide, anxiety, hopelessness, and depression, this book will help you. Surprisingly, the answer to these and many other challenges has been around for thousands of years. If you're looking for hope, peace, happiness, prosperity, wisdom, and the fullness of life, look no further.

Book Of Proverbs: Proverbs For The Modern Day delves deeply into the timeless human quest for wisdom. As all Christians know, the primary purpose of the Biblical Book of Proverbs is to teach wisdom. The Book of Proverbs provides intellectual depth, insights, and exceptional wisdom on how to live a meaningful, joyful, and tranquil life by honoring and respecting God as omnipotent.

This updated version of Book Of Proverbs: Proverbs For The Modern Day discusses all chapters in Proverbs 1-31 and brings insight, clarity, and basic meaning to several verses in each chapter. It clarifies why wisdom is not only essential, but mandatory in life, if one hopes to live a blessed life, versus living destitute, empty, or feeling lost or hopeless.

https://amzn.to/46DUKJt

The Rain Falls On The Just And The Unjust

As much as Christians or believers of God would like to believe that just because we acknowledge God in our lives, we should have no sorrow that is untrue. Just believing this makes us commit sin, because then we are not humble but haughty. We will all have challenges, disappointments, and unfair situations arise in our lives, but as believers of God, we are to handle ourselves so that unbelievers will want to become like us. We are to TRUST, HAVE FAITH, and BELIEVE that GOD has our back and will keep us lifted above, fight our battles, and always cause us to triumph!

https://amzn.to/46DUKJt

Thriving In Every Season Of Life With God

From multi award-winning author Donna Louis, Thriving In Every Season Of Life With God gives us a road map to create a mindset, a new life in which we can learn to prosper in any circumstance.

To understand what it means to "thrive," we must look beyond the dimension of finances. The concept of thriving can apply to our health, our relationships, our habits and our peace of mind. God wants us to thrive. But it does not just happen - we must take action to make it happen.

Set against the backdrop of four "seasons of life", Louis, in the tradition of writers such as Joel Osteen, discusses how you can thrive, prosper, and flourish. Much like growing crops, we prepare in spring, grow in summer, harvest in fall and rest in winter. At times we must nurture and cultivate, at other times we bloom and reproduce, and at other times we harvest and replant.

Thriving In Every Season Of Life With God is a book that can be read in just a few hours and provides readers with powerful ideas and concepts that can be implemented immediately, allowing them to thrive amid adversity.

https://amzn.to/46DUKJt

Miracles of Direction, Miracles of Conquest, Miracles of Provision, Miracles of Purpose

Do you dare to dream?

Do you dare to believe that miracles are possible?

Everyday miracles are happening all around us in every shape, form, and fashion.

The miracle birth of a two-headed turtle, Capt. Chesley B. Sullenberger who safely landed US Airways Flight 1549 in the Hudson River after the plane hit a flock of geese and lost power - saving the lives of all 155 people on board, and motivational speaker Nick Vujicic who was born without arms or legs who can do just about everything.

Miracles of Direction, Miracles of Conquest, Miracles of Provision, and Miracles of Purpose delves into biblical miracles that took place while Jesus was here on earth and cross references with miracles that take place daily now in the 21st century.

In the book there is a biblical character Gideon, who takes the first step and obeys the lord when he speaks to him and is ultimately given victory in a war when he downsized his army from 32,000 men to 300 versus the Midianites.

"Take the first step in faith. You don't have to see the whole staircase. Just take the first step." Dr. Martin Luther King 1929-1968.

https://amzn.to/46DUKJt

www.ingramcontent.com/pod-product-compliance
Lightning Source LLC
Chambersburg PA
CBHW051333150726
47997CB00004B/1454